The Colors We Eat

Black Foods

Isabel Thomas

Heinemann Library
Chicago, Illinois

Customer Service   888–454–2279
Visit our website at www.heinemannlibrary.com

Printed and bound in china by South China Printing Co. Ltd.

09 08 07 06 05
10 9 8 7 6 5 4 3 2 1

Library of Congress Cataloging-in-Publication Data
 Thomas, Isabel, 1980-
  Black foods / Isabel Thomas.
      p. cm. -- (The colors we eat)
  Includes index.
  ISBN 1-4034-6315-8 (hc) -- ISBN 1-4034-6322-0 (pbk.)
 1. Food--Juvenile literature. 2. Black--Juvenile literature. I.
Title. II. Series.
  TX355.T4525 2004
  641.3--dc22

                    2004005219

Acknowledgments
The author and publisher are grateful to the following for permission to reproduce copyright material:
pp. 4, 5, 6, 7, 10, 11, 12, 13, 14, 15, 16, 17, 18, 19, 20, 21, 21 Tudor Photography/Heinemann Library; p. 8 David Mardsen/Anthony Blake Photo Library; p. 9 Gordon Maclean/OSF; p. 23 (root) Richard Shiell/OSF.

Cover photograph: Tudor Photography/Heinemann Library

Every effort has been made to contact copyright holders of any material reproduced in this book. Any omissions will be rectified in subsequent printings if notice is given to the publisher.

Special thanks to our advisory panel for their help in the preparation of this book:

Alice Bethke,
Library Consultant
Palo Alto, CA

Eileen Day,
Preschool Teacher
Chicago, IL

Sandra Gilbert,
Library Media Specialist
Fiest Elementary School
Houston, TX

Jan Gobeille,
Kindergarten Teacher
Garfield Elementary
Oakland, CA

Angela Leeper,
Educational Consultant
Wake Forest, NC

Melinda Murphy,
Library Media Specialist
Houston, TX

Some words are shown in bold, **like this.**
You can find them in the glossary on page 23.

Contents

Have You Eaten Black Foods?. 4

What Are Some Small Black Foods?. 6

What Are Some Other Small
Black Foods? 8

What Are Some Tiny Black Foods?. 10

What Are Some Crunchy
Black Foods? 12

What Are Some Chewy
Black Foods? 14

What Are Some Strange
Black Foods? 16

What Are Some Black Liquids? 18

Black and Green Fruit Salad Recipe 20

Quiz 22

Picture Glossary 23

Note to Parents and Teachers 24

Answers to Quiz. 24

Index 24

Have You Eaten Black Foods?

Colors are all around us.

You might have eaten some of these colors.

There are black fruits and vegetables.

There are other black foods, too.

What Are Some Small Black Foods?

Some grapes are small and black.

Grapes grow in bunches on **vines**.

Some beans are small and black.

Beans grow in pods.

What Are Some Other Small Black Foods?

Black currants are small berries.

Some people use them to make jam.

Blackberries are sweet and juicy.

They grow on bushes.

What Are Some Tiny Black Foods?

Sunflower seeds have black and white stripes.

Birds love to eat them.

Poppy seeds are tiny.

You might see them on top
of **bagels**.

What Are Some Crunchy Black Foods?

Peppercorns are tiny, dried fruits.

We **grind** peppercorns up to make black pepper.

Some rice **grains** are black.

Rice is hard and crunchy.

We cook rice to make it soft.

What Are Some Chewy Black Foods?

Licorice is a soft, chewy candy.

Its **flavor** comes from a dry **root**.

plum

grape

prune

raisin

Raisins are chewy, dried grapes.

Prunes are chewy, dried plums.

What Are Some Strange Black Foods?

Vanilla beans are long and thin.

They are used to add **flavor** to foods.

Olives are a fruit.

Olive oil is squeezed out of olives.

What Are Some Black Liquids?

Soy sauce is used in cooking.

It is made from soya beans.

Some kinds of molasses are black.

Some people use it to make cakes.

Black And Green Fruit Salad Recipe

Ask an adult to help you.

First, cut up some black grapes, kiwifruits, and passion fruits.

Next, mix everything in a bowl.

Add grape juice and yogurt.

Then eat your black and green fruit salad.

Quiz

Can you name these black foods?

Look for the answers on page 24.

Picture Glossary

bagel
page 11
type of bread that is round and has a hole in the middle

flavor
pages 14, 16
taste of a food

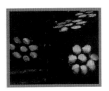
grain
page 13
tiny fruit of a plant like rice

grind
page 12
crush something into small bits

root
page 14
part of a plant that grows underground

vine
page 6
bush that grapes or olives grow on

Note to Parents and Teachers

Reading for information is an important part of a child's literacy development. Learning begins with a question about something. Help children think of themselves as investigators and researchers by encouraging their questions about the world around them. Each chapter in this book begins with a question. Read the question together. Look at the pictures. Talk about what you think the answer might be. Then read the text to find out if your predictions were correct. Think of other questions you could ask about the topic, and discuss where you might find the answers. Assist children in using the picture glossary and the index to practice new vocabulary and research skills.

Index

bean 7
blackberry 9
black currant 8
grape 6, 15, 20
kiwifruit 20
licorice 14
olive 17
passion fruit 20
peppercorn 12
plum 15
poppy seed 11
prune 15
rice 13
soy sauce 18
sunflower seed 10
vanilla bean 16

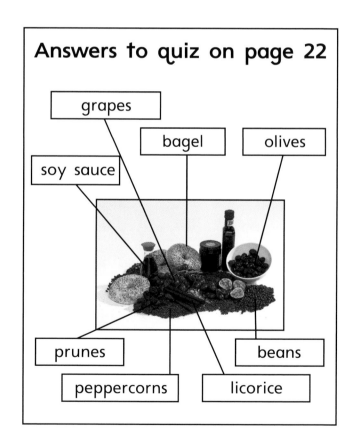

Answers to quiz on page 22

grapes

bagel

olives

soy sauce

prunes

beans

peppercorns

licorice